Are You a REPTILE?

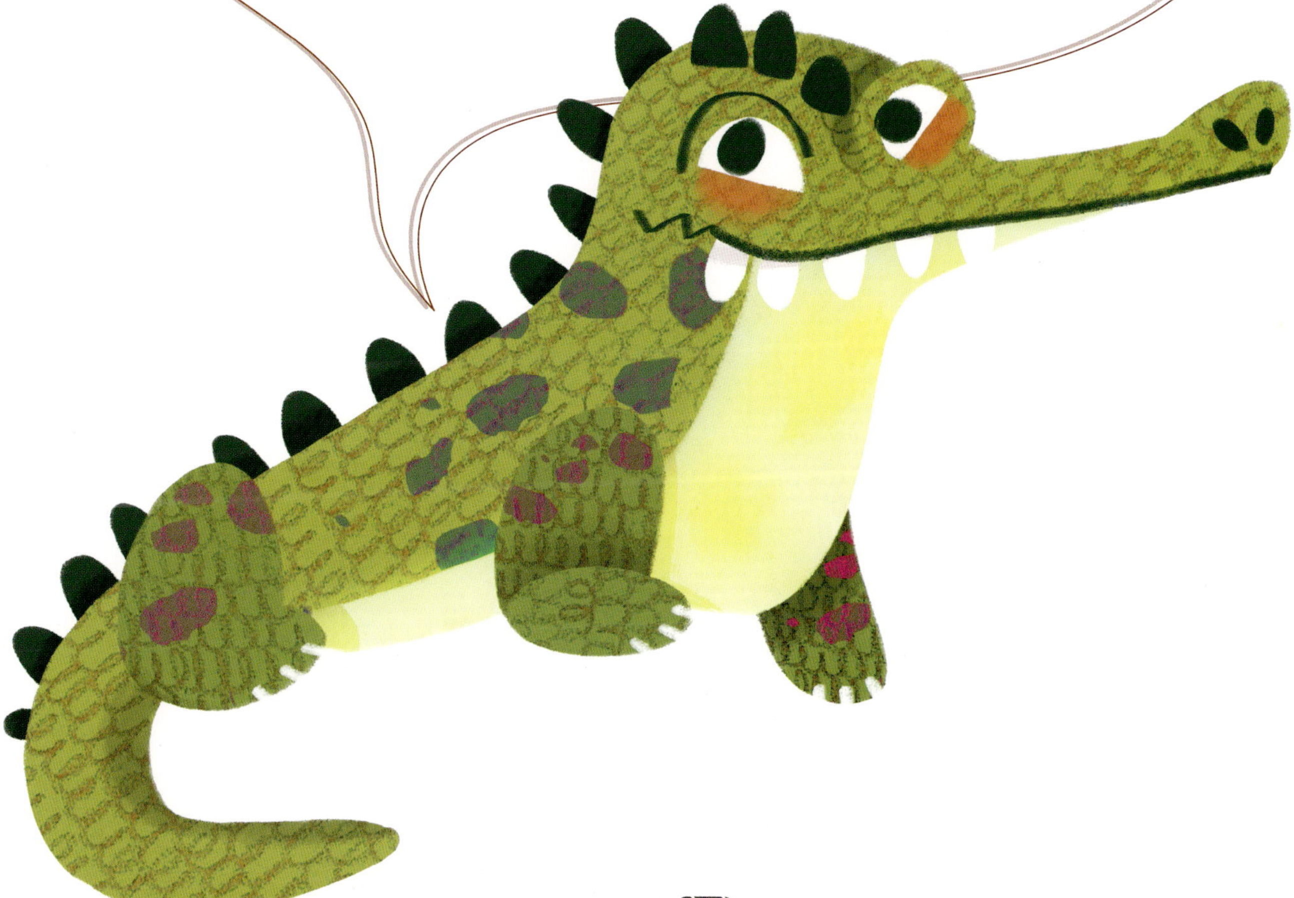

by THOMAS KINGSLEY TROUPE

illustrated by MARTINA ROTONDO

Allison was an alligator. Last Monday, she heard an interesting word.

"There might be reptiles nearby, kids," Marty the mouse said.

"What's a reptile?" Allison asked.

"I knew it!" Marty cried. "Run for your lives!" The mice squeaked and ran away.

Allison didn't know what Marty knew.
But she DID want to know what a reptile was.

Allison crawled into the river to look for reptiles.
Allison asked Belinda the bass.

"A reptile?" Belinda said.
"Oh, no, toothy one. I have gills. Reptiles have lungs."
"What do lungs do?" Allison asked.
"They help reptiles breathe oxygen,"
Belinda said. "All reptiles have at
least one lung."
Allison made a note about lungs.

Allison found Preston the pig.

Preston grunted. "No ma'am," he said. "I'm warm-blooded. Reptiles are cold-blooded. They can't keep their body temperature the same like I can."

"That's not good," Allison replied.

"Right," Preston agreed.
"If the temperature is too cold or
too hot, it's trouble for them!"

Allison wrote cold-blooded in her notebook.

Allison spotted Rusty the rooster.

"Are you a reptile?" Allison asked.
"I am not!" Rusty crowed. "What's
wrong with cock-a-doodle you?
Reptiles have tails!"
"Don't you?" Allison asked.
"Well, I do," Rusty said. "But my tail
has feathers. Reptiles' tails don't!"

Allison made notes about tails
without feathers.

Allison saw Winona the worm.

"Is this some kind of a joke?"
Winona replied.
"I'm no reptile. I'm not a vertebrate!"

"A vertebrate? What does that mean?" Allison asked.

"I don't have a backbone or even a skeleton," Winona said. "But all reptiles do!"

Allison wrote down some vertebrate facts.

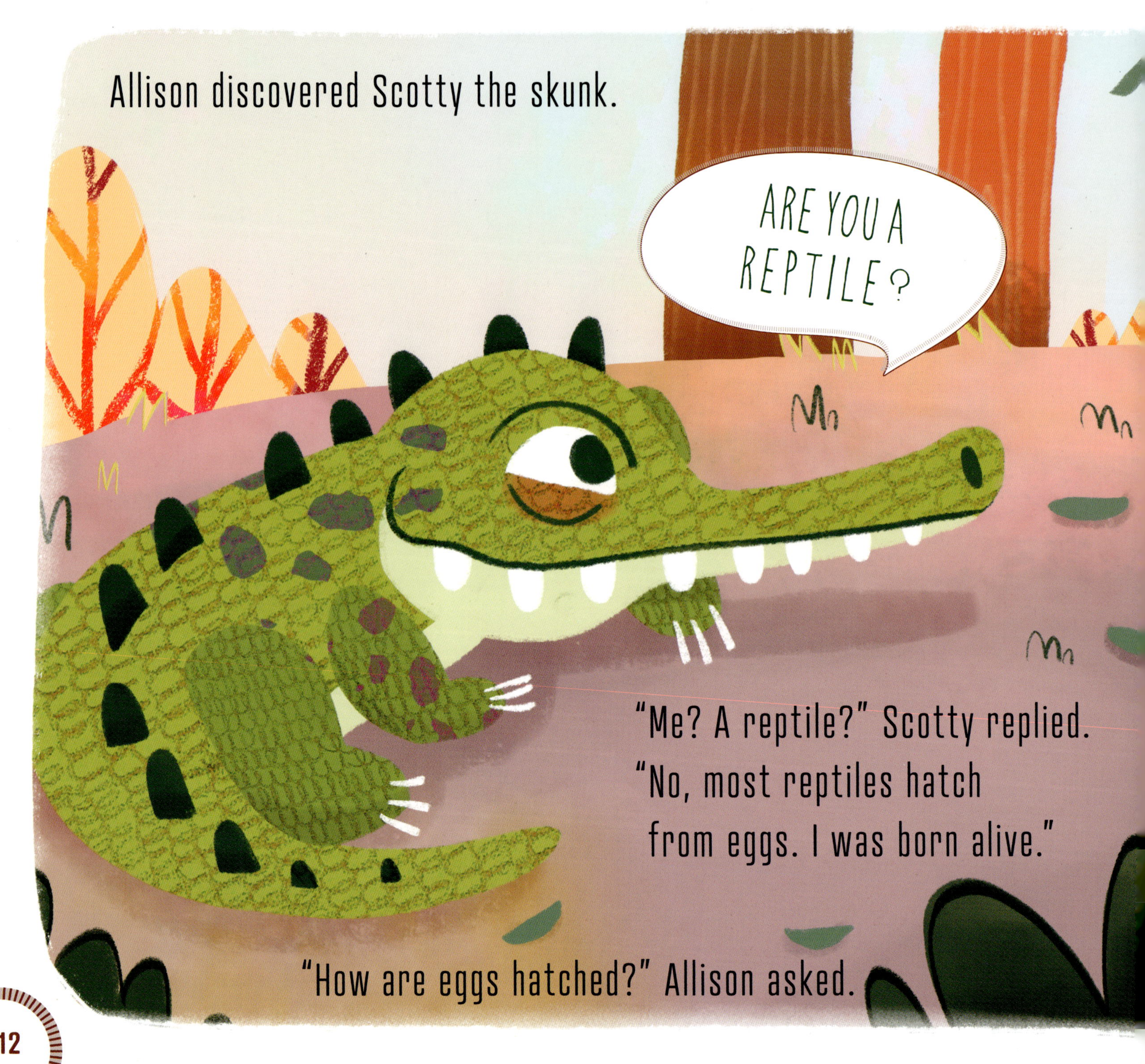

Allison discovered Scotty the skunk.

"Me? A reptile?" Scotty replied.
"No, most reptiles hatch
from eggs. I was born alive."

"How are eggs hatched?" Allison asked.

"They're kept warm and dry until they're ready to break open," Scotty explained. "Then, little reptiles pop out."

Allison added eggs to her list.

Allison caught up with Nadia the newt.

"Not quite, Scratchy," Nadia replied.
"My nice skin is moist and smooth."

"Isn't reptile skin like that?" Allison asked.

"Oh no," Nadia said. "Almost all reptiles have rough, scaly skin."

Allison scribbled rough and scaly skin in her notepad.

Allison met Rashida the rabbit.

"Are you a reptile?" Allison asked.
"Who me? A reptile?" Rashida replied.
"No, no, no. See these big ears on
  my head?"
"Reptiles don't have ears?" Allison asked.
"Not all do, no," Rashida explained.
"But it's hard to see the ears on reptiles
  that do have them. Their ears don't
  stick out."

Allison made notes about ears.

Allison came across Talulah the turtle. She saw her moving along the swamp.

"Umm," Allison began.

"I sure am, sister," Talulah laughed. "Almost all reptiles have scales on their body like I do."

"They help protect me from predators. They keep me from drying up."

"All right!" Allison cried. "I found a reptile!"

Allison followed Talulah through the cattails. There, she saw other reptiles with rough, scaly skin. They were breathing air. She didn't see any big ears.

"Are you all reptiles?"

"We ssssure are, sssssmart one," Sissy the snake hissed. "And you are too!"

Allison looked at herself. She had scales and a tail. She had a backbone and her ears were hidden. She was a reptile too!

"I should've known!" Allison shouted and smiled.

Allison's Notebook

REPTILES . . .

- Use lungs to breathe oxygen.

- Are cold-blooded. Their body temperature is the same as their surroundings.

- Have tails (no feathers!)

- Are vertebrates. They have a backbone.

- Hatch from eggs (most of them). The eggs need to be kept dry and warm.

- Have rough, scaly skin.

- Don't have large ear openings that can be easily seen.

- Have scales covering their bodies.

GLOSSARY

cold-blooded Having a body temperature that changes to match the surrounding temperature.

lung An organ inside an animal's body that helps it breathe air.

oxygen A colorless gas in the air that animals need to breathe.

scale One of the thin, flat, overlapping pieces of hard skin that cover a reptile's body.

vertebrate An animal that has a backbone and a skeleton of bones inside its body.

warm-blooded Having a body temperature that stays about the same no matter what the surounding temperature is.

WEBSITES

National Wildlife Federation: Reptiles

https://www.nwf.org/Educational-Resources/Wildlife-Guide/Reptiles

Reptiles: National Geographic Kids

https://kids.nationalgeographic.com/animals/reptiles

Reptiles | San Diego Zoo Animals and Plants

https://animals.sandiegozoo.org/animals/reptiles

Every effort has been made to ensure that these websites are appropriate for children. However, because of the nature of the Internet, it is impossible to guarantee that these sites will remain active indefinitely or that their contents will not be altered.

READ MORE

Jaycox, Jaclyn. *Unusual Life Cycles of Reptiles.* North Mankato, Minn.: Pebble, an imprint of Capstone, 2021.

Rathburn, Betsy. *Remarkable Reptiles.* Minneapolis: Bellwether Media, 2023.

Vonder Brink, Tracy. *Reptiles.* Crabtree Publishing: New York, 2023.

AMICUS ILLUSTRATED is published by
Amicus Learning, an imprint of Amicus
P.O. Box 227, Mankato, MN 56002
www.amicuspublishing.us

Library of Congress Cataloging-in-Publication Data
Names: Troupe, Thomas Kingsley, author. | Rotondo, Martina, illustrator.
Title: Are you a reptile? / by Thomas Kingsley Troupe ; illustrated by Martina Rotondo.
Description: Mankato, MN : Amicus Illustrated, [2025] | Series: Animal classification | Includes bibliographical references. | Audience: Ages 6–9 | Audience: Grades 2–3 | Summary: "When young Allison the alligator hears Marty the mouse warning his friends to run away from reptiles, Allison sets out on a mission to find out what exactly a reptile is. After interviewing other animals and learning about the characteristics of reptiles, Allison realizes that she too is a reptile! Includes fact page, glossary, and resources for further research" — Provided by publisher.
Identifiers: LCCN 2024010608 (print) | LCCN 2024010609 (ebook) | ISBN 9798892001182 (library binding) | ISBN 9798892001762 (paperback) | ISBN 9798892002349 (ebook)
Subjects: LCSH: Reptiles—Juvenile literature. | Reptiles—Classification—Juvenile literature. | Animals—Classification—Juvenile literature.
Classification: LCC QL644.2 .T763 2025 (print) | LCC QL644.2 (ebook) | DDC 597.901/2—dc23/eng/20240405
LC record available at https://lccn.loc.gov/2024010608
LC ebook record available at https://lccn.loc.gov/2024010609

Printed in China

Editor: Rebecca Glaser
Designer: Kim Pfeffer

ABOUT THE AUTHOR

Thomas Kingsley Troupe is the author of more than 200 books for young readers. When he's not writing, he enjoys reading, playing video games, and investigating haunted places with the Twin Cities Paranormal Society. Otherwise, he's probably taking a nap or something. Thomas lives in Woodbury, Minnesota, with his two sons.

ABOUT THE ILLUSTRATOR

Artist since always, Martina Rotondo attended the Master of Illustration and Concept Art at The Sign Academy in Florence, Italy. She currently works as an illustrator for both Italian and foreign publishing houses. Lover of traditional drawing, she is also constantly researching and experimenting with new techniques to create her surreal and engaging characters and backgrounds.